# CATS: 101 Amazing Cat Facts

## CAT FACTS FOR KIDS!

## JENNY KELLETT

ISBN-13: 978-1516911875
ISBN-10: 1516911873

# INTRODUCTION

Thank you for buying my latest book. As a lifelong cat lover, I had so much fun researching and writing this book and I hope you enjoy reading it!

My gorgeous kitties Billy and Bella (above and opposite) are my inspiration and are always keeps me company while I'm writing.

A cat's nose has a unique ridged pattern, just like a human fingerprint.

----------

When cats are in a bad mood, they thrash their tails back and forth - so it's a good idea to leave her alone! Dogs do this when they're happy.

----------

Cats spend around 30 per cent of their time awake cleaning themselves.

----------

Cats are able to make over 100 different sounds, whereas dogs can only make 10.

----------

Cats cannot move their jaws sideways

----------

Cats often squeeze their eyes shut when they are happy

----------

Ever wondered why they don't sell mouse-flavored cat food? When scientists tested it, cats didn't like it!

----------

A cat's average body temperature is warmer than human's at around 101.5 F (38.6 Celsius).

Cats can turn their ears 180 degrees

---------

Adult cats have 32 teeth - 16 on the top;
14 on the bottom.

---------

Cats are very lazy - they sleep around 16 hours a day!     8

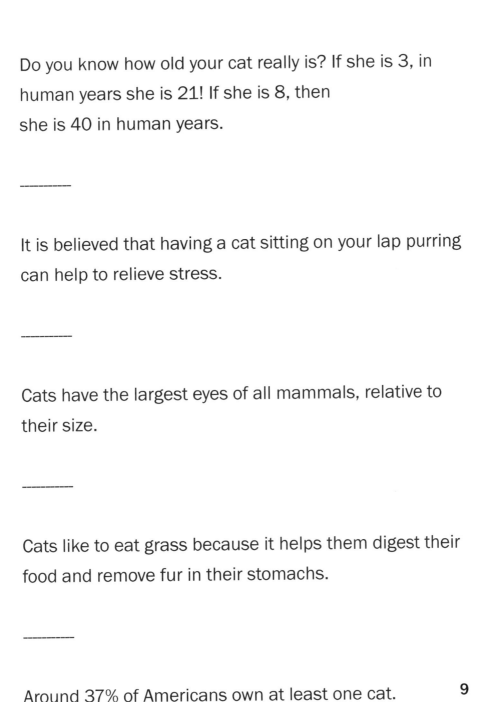

Do you know how old your cat really is? If she is 3, in human years she is 21! If she is 8, then she is 40 in human years.

_____

It is believed that having a cat sitting on your lap purring can help to relieve stress.

_____

Cats have the largest eyes of all mammals, relative to their size.

_____

Cats like to eat grass because it helps them digest their food and remove fur in their stomachs.

_____

Around 37% of Americans own at least one cat.

Domestic cats can run up to 30 miles per hour!

--------

Cats with blue eyes and white fur are often deaf

--------

Cats use their tails to balance themselves

--------

Cats have very sensitive hearing - more sensitive than humans and dogs

--------

Female cats are usually pregnant for around 9 weeks compared to humans, who are pregnant for 9 months!

--------

The official name for cat lovers is an Ailurophile! Are you an Ailurophile?

Cats not only purr when they are happy, they can also purr when they are in pain.

————

When your cat rubs up against you it means she is claiming ownership of you - so take it as a compliment!

Cats are lactose intolerant - this means that you shouldn't give them cow's milk, cheese or chocolate as it can make them very sick.

---------

Ancient Egyptians believed that 'Bast' was the mover of all cats on Earth. They also believed that cats were sacred.

---------

Durings its life, a female cat could have more than 100 kittens.

---------

Sir Isaac Newton, who discovered gravity, also invented the cat flap!

---------

The most popular names for cats in America are Missy, Misty, Muffin, Patches, Fluffy, Tabitha, Tigger, Pumpkin and Samantha. Is yours on the list?

If your cat likes to climb your Christmas tree, try hanging a lemon or orange scented air freshener in the branches - cats don't like this smell.

----------

Cats are slightly color-blind - they can't tell the difference between green and red.

Cats' vision isn't that good at seeing detail - you will probably appear blurry to them.

----------

The color of a kitten's eyes changes as it gets older.

----------

When kittens are first born, they can't see or hear. Their eyes open at five days old and their hearing and sight is developed when they are around two weeks old.

A group of adult cats is called a 'clowder'.

---------

Cats can't be vegetarians - they need protein from meat to survive.

---------

Never feed your cat dog food, cats require five times more protein than dogs to stay healthy

---------

The average cat weighs 12 pounds. How much does yours weigh?

---------

Cats are considered to be overweight if you can't feel their ribs.

The smallest cat ever recorded was Tinker Toy from Illinois. He weighed 1 pound and 8 ounces and was just 2.75 inches tall!

_____

A cat's normal pulse is 140-240 beats per minute, with an average of 195. This is nearly twice as fast a a human.

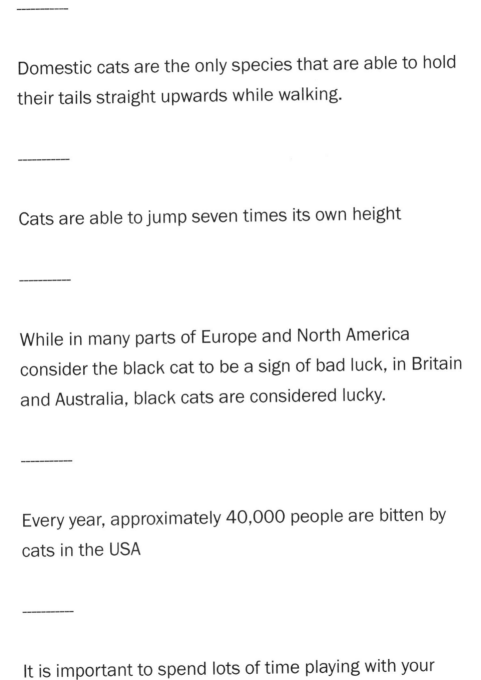

----------

Domestic cats are the only species that are able to hold their tails straight upwards while walking.

----------

Cats are able to jump seven times its own height

----------

While in many parts of Europe and North America consider the black cat to be a sign of bad luck, in Britain and Australia, black cats are considered lucky.

----------

Every year, approximately 40,000 people are bitten by cats in the USA

----------

It is important to spend lots of time playing with your kitten when he or she is very young so that they don't develop a fear of people.

Female cats can begin mating when they are between five and nine months old.

---------

All domestic cats have the same ancestor - the African Wild Cat - which still exists today.

---------

Cats can be both right-pawed and left-pawed, just like humans.

Cats are the only animals that have retractable claws.

---------

If your cat snores or rolls over and show you her belly, it means she trusts you.

---------

The Ancient Egyptian word for cat was 'mau', which means 'to see'.

Kittens, just like humans, are born with baby teeth which are replaced by permanent teeth when they around seven months old.

_____

Cats cannot see directly under their noses.

Cats take between 20-40 breaths a minute

----------

There are around 100 different breeds of cats.

Scottish Fold cats have cute fold-over ears!

----------

Cats can live for more than 20 years, but on average they live for 14 years.

----------

Just like humans, cats can get asthma. Dust, smoke and other air pollution can irritate your cat.

----------

Cats that have long, lean bodies are more likely to be outgoing, whereas stocky cats are more protective and vocal.

A cat's brain is more similar to a human brain than a dog brain

---------

Cats rarely meow at other cats, they only meow to humans. They spit, purr and hiss at other cats.

---------

The Pilgrims were the first to introduce cats to North America.

---------

A cat called Dusty is recorded as having the most number of kittens - she had 420 in her lifetime.

---------

In 1987, cats overtook dogs as the most popular pet in America.

---------

Almost 10 per cent of a cat's bones are in its tail

The world's first cat show was in London in 1871. The first one in America was in 1895.

--------

Cats step with both left legs, then both right legs when they walk or run.

The world's richest cat was Blackie, who was left $20 million by his owner who passed away.

----------

Cats walk on their toes.

----------

Cats' tongues have tiny barbs on them.

----------

Cats can't taste sweet things.

----------

Most cats have no eyelashes.

----------

Be careful what plants your cat gets to, as many are poisonous to them! English Ivy, Iris, Mistletoe and Yew are all poisonous to cats.

Cats bury their poo to hide their scent from predators.

--------

Kittens are taught to use a litter tray by their mothers, so it's important they stay with their mothers until they are at least nine weeks old.

Unlike humans, cats do not need to blink regularly to keep their eyes lubricated.

--------

Even some of the scariest men in history were afraid of cats! Julius Caesar, Charles XI and Henry II all had a phobia of cats.

--------

Even when cats are sleeping they can tell when they are being touched. Trying touching your cats tail as she is sleeping and you'll see her twitch!

Cats are more likely to respond to a name that ends in the sound 'ee'.

----------

Abraham Lincoln loved cats - he had four of them living with him at the White House.

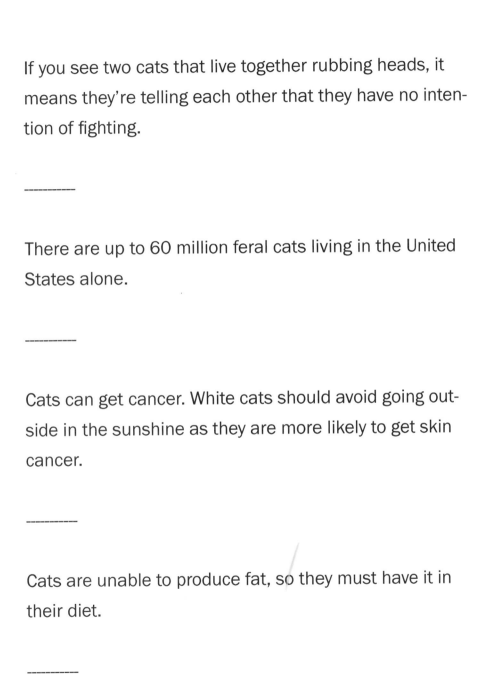

If you see two cats that live together rubbing heads, it means they're telling each other that they have no intention of fighting.

----------

There are up to 60 million feral cats living in the United States alone.

----------

Cats can get cancer. White cats should avoid going outside in the sunshine as they are more likely to get skin cancer.

----------

Cats are unable to produce fat, so they must have it in their diet.

----------

Cats have around 130,000 hairs per square inch!

It is believed that cats don't think that they are little people, instead they see humans as big cats!

--------

Cats can be taught to walk on a leash, but it takes time and is easiest if you start them off when they are very young.

--------

On average, cats have 24 whiskers; four horizontal rows on each side of their faces.

--------

By having your cat neutered, it can increase their lifespan by up to three years.

--------

Cats are able to predict when earthquakes will happen. Scientists aren't sure why, but they are studying it at the moment.

Cats can't move their jaws sideways, which is why they can't eat large chunks of food. Always make sure your cats food is well chopped up.

----------

Cats can drink around 5 teaspoons of water or milk every minute.

It is estimated that around 54 per cent of cats in America are overweight. Make sure you feed your cat a healthy diet, rich in protein and low in fat. A typical cat only needs around 180-200 calories each day.

----------

Your cat's front paws have five toes, whereas the back paws only have four.

----------

Cats can hear the ultrasonic sounds that mice make, which helps them when hunting.

----------

A cat's collar bone is not connected to any other bones, it is surrounded by muscle. This makes it easy for them to squeeze through tight spots.

----------

Cats only have 473 taste buds; humans have over 9,000.

Cats can tell when you are angry at them by the tone of your voice.

----------

Cats purr 26 times per second, which is why you hear the buzzing sound

----------

When cats are really happy, they knead their paws.

----------

In the Macy's Thanksgiving Day parade, a Felix the Cat balloon was the first balloon ever used.

# CATS & KITTENS
# CROSSWORD

| C | A | T | S | G | H | E | S | A | B | G | D |
|---|---|---|---|---|---|---|---|---|---|---|---|
| R | L | W | M | A | N | X | F | G | U | S | H |
| H | I | G | A | U | K | A | L | H | R | P | R |
| F | T | E | H | T | I | H | U | J | M | E | D |
| E | T | D | R | E | T | D | F | G | E | R | H |
| G | E | A | W | G | T | E | F | S | S | S | O |
| K | R | T | I | G | E | R | Y | N | E | I | S |
| Y | P | F | A | S | N | T | R | R | S | A | T |
| F | F | S | B | R | S | S | F | U | R | N | A |
| D | S | I | A | M | E | S | E | P | F | A | I |
| W | H | I | S | K | E | R | S | Q | J | S | L |
| A | H | F | S | E | H | K | T | H | W | G | R |

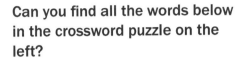

Can you find all the words below
in the crossword puzzle on the
left?

| | |
|---|---|
| CATS | FLUFFY |
| KITTENS | SIAMESE |
| BURMESE | TIGER |
| FUR | LITTER |
| TAIL | MANX |
| WHISKERS | PERSIAN |

CPSIA information can be obtained at www.ICGtesting.com
Printed in the USA
BVIW12n1156181217
503087BV00034B/490